Life Lines

THE LANIER PHILLIPS STORY

CHRISTINE WELLDON

P.O. Box 2188, St. John's, NL, Canada, A1C 6E6
WWW.BREAKWATERBOOKS.COM

LIBRARY AND ARCHIVES CANADA CATALOGUING IN PUBLICATION
Welldon, Christine, author
Life lines : the story of Lanier Phillips / Christine Welldon.
ISBN 978-1-55081-551-1 (bound)

1. Phillips, Lanier, 1923-2012--Juvenile literature.
2. African American civil rights workers--Biography--Juvenile literature.
3. African American soldiers--Biography--Juvenile literature.
4. St. Lawrence (N.L.)--Biography--Juvenile literature. I. Title.
E185.97.P45W45 2014   305.896'073   C2014-901922-X

  Canada Council Conseil des Arts   Canadä   Newfoundland
for the Arts   du Canada   Labrador

We acknowledge the support of the Canada Council for the Arts, which last year
invested $157 million to bring the arts to Canadians throughout the country. We
acknowledge the financial support of the Government of Canada through the
Canada Book Fund (CBF) and the Government of Newfoundland and Labrador
through the Department of Tourism, Culture and Recreation for our publishing
activities.

PRINTED AND BOUND IN CANADA.

Breakwater Books is committed to choosing papers and materials for our
books that help to protect our environment. To this end, this book is printed
on a recycled paper that is certified by the Forest Stewardship Council®.

RECYCLED
Paper made from
recycled material
FSC
www.fsc.org   FSC® C103567

**Dedicated to the people
of St. Lawrence and Lawn.**

Table of Contents

Foreword

When I began to write this book, one well-placed call linked me to many people who loved Lanier Phillips and his legacy. These, of course, are the people of St. Lawrence and Lawn. I received an immediate response from so many kind-hearted and helpful souls who wanted to talk about Dr. Phillips. It is no wonder that his friendship with these strong and resourceful Newfoundlanders was so enduring. My text is based on historical facts, anecdotes, and archival research. At the beginning of each chapter, I have written a historically accurate narrative based on Lanier Phillips' recorded interviews. I owe a special thank you to Mayor Wayde Rowsell, the fulcrum of my network, for his tireless efforts in providing anecdotes and images, to help me explore and celebrate Dr. Phillips' life. My own life has been enriched by these connections.

Never a Kind Word

THE YEAR WAS 1932. The boy crouched in the ditch at the side of the road. He listened as a freight train rumbled by, its noise fading into the hot night air. There was stillness once again, but it was a hushed, waiting kind of stillness, as though all the creatures of the night listened with him. Then he heard it—the sound of marching steps coming along Main Street toward the railway track. Marching toward him.

He ducked lower, scarcely breathing.

Which way would the Klan go?

Across the tracks and straight on meant they were not going to make trouble in his street tonight. If they turned right, he would need to run like a rabbit to warn his folks.

Left, right, left, right, went the marching steps. The men were near his hiding place, and he could hear the sounds of muttered words, the metallic clink of guns and knives hidden in their robes. He daren't look up.

They went on by and he got up from his crouch and sprinted through the woods, running at an angle that would take him on a shortcut to the edge of Pendley Street. If they turned onto Pendley, it meant sure trouble. He crouched behind the bushes that lined the street there and waited for them.

Which way?

Their hollow footsteps rang softer as they left the concrete road and took the dirt road to the right. So it was to be his street tonight! His heart jumped in his chest like a startled cat. As soon as they passed, he sprinted back into the trees as quietly as he could, taking the quick and short path that would lead him behind the row of homes where his family lived.

He was behind old man Bruce's house now. The lamps were already out, there. The two grandsons waited in the yard to catch sight of him. "They coming, Lanier?"

"Yes, they're coming!" he called to them as he ran by.

The boys would pass the message along. He ran through his yard, past the old oak tree with the rope swing, seeing the lamps lit in the back room.

"Turn out the lamps! They're coming!" he yelled. But his grandfather was already snuffing out the candles. Just the look on Lanier's face as he ran through the kitchen door was enough to know.

Lanier was frightened much of the time, but he tried never to show it. Mostly, he listened and watched, all his senses on alert. Whether he was approaching the corner on Main where the smirking White kids leaned against the wall, or heading home from school on a route that was especially full of taunts and tricks, he was as careful as any Black boy only nine years old could be.

At the beginning of each day, his mother told him, "Stay out of trouble. Never look a White boy in the face else you'll get a whipping or a lynching."

At day's end, his grandfather might find cause to chide him. "Your ma told you to be careful, boy, and now look at you."

Through it all, Lanier tried to stay safe.

The crash of breaking glass struck a new terror. His mother dropped the cup she held, and Lanier bent to pick it up, but she gently pushed him away. Lanier's brothers and sisters stood poised to run, and their mother herded them toward the back room.

"Get up to the attic," she said.

Lanier did as she asked, propping up the ladder and lifting the trap door in the ceiling. His younger brothers and sisters climbed up first, then Lanier. "You come too!" he hissed, but his mother was bolting the front door and hustling his grandmother away from the window.

The children could hear shouts and taunts from the street, the staccato pop, pop of guns intermingled with the sound of a woman's cries. Lanier told his brothers and sisters to cover their ears. He did the same. He curled up into a ball, hearing his breathing come fast and ragged, waiting for it all to stop.

He drifted into sleep. When he awoke, there was only silence, as though the neighbourhood held its breath. The Klan's game of terror was over for tonight.

• • •

The Ku Klux Klan is a membership of lawless people who use terror to do their work. In Lanier's time, they were much stronger than they are today. White supremacy has always been one of their goals.

Back in 1863, after the American Civil War, President Abraham Lincoln freed all slaves and abolished slavery, but he could not abolish racism. The ugly shadows of racial prejudice stayed. African Americans now had the freedom to move away from the

Charles T. Webber's *The Underground Railroad* (1893) depicts a group of slaves travelling toward freedom.

South to wherever they felt safest, but none were able to escape racial hatred. Even those freed slaves who migrated north to Canada did not find peace from racism.

Over the years to follow, the Klan lynched thousands of African Americans—terrorizing them, burning their homes, and randomly killing them. White robes and flaming crosses were symbols of violence toward Black people.

In 1923, during this time of racial hatred and fear, Lanier Walter Phillips was born in the small town of Lithonia, Georgia. Here, as in other towns, the Ku Klux Klan owned and ran everything from the village store to the police station. There was no escaping its power.

"In fact, all the White people were Klan as far as I knew. They all were Klan, and they all were racists—utmost racists," Lanier said. He remembered the time a man had slashed his mother's tires, and the time people used their truck to push her car off the road after she ran out of gas. "I never heard a kind word from a White man in my life," recalled Lanier.

The Ku Klux Klan's Grand Dragon standing with children during an initiation ceremony in 1948. The KKK are a White supremacist group who preach hate towards people of other races.

Lanier's childhood was not much different from that of other African-American children who lived in the southern United States. At the store, on the street, in the playground, there was never a time when he felt safe from racial hatred.

By law, Black children must not play with White children. They were not allowed to play baseball within two blocks of a playground for White children. They must not attend the same church. They must not use the same water fountains as Whites, and they must only use the public toilets that had signs for "Coloreds" on the wall. Schoolbooks shared by White children were not to be used by Black children. Black people must not be buried in the same cemetery as Whites.

It is no wonder the White children looked down on the children of African descent and made them feel worthless. Their parents taught them to judge other people first by the colour of their skin, and they grew up believing that, because they were White, they were better in every way. It is also no wonder that children like Lanier spent their childhoods in fear and hatred of Whites. If anything went wrong, people blamed African Americans and punished them with mob violence and murder.

Sharecroppers chopping cotton.

When Lanier's great-grandmother and grandfather were freed from slavery, they stayed on in Georgia earning a living as sharecroppers on farms. Like other freed slaves, they rented shares—small pieces of land—grew crops, and gave their harvest to the White landowners.

Lanier's mother and father were sharecroppers too, and Lanier expected to do the same work when he was grown up. There were almost two million sharecroppers in the south, and their lives were not much different than they had been during slavery.

Landowner bosses were often very poor managers or too lazy to care. Cotton crops could fail because of drought, plant disease, or bad weather. Sharecroppers earned only pennies each month and often had to move on and work somewhere else after only a year. The same things went wrong wherever they went. It was a miserable life of hunger and poverty.

When Lanier was six years old, the African-American people of three Georgia counties worked together to save money to build a school, the first ever for their children. They knew the importance of education and that learning to read and write would help to empower them, give their children a chance to better themselves. The Klan knew it too and smashed their hopes once again. They set fire to the school.

Lanier remembered seeing the flames, feeling the heat on his cheeks as the Yellow River School burned to the ground.

"They'll never let our children learn to read," said his mother. She expressed the despair of so many African-American parents whose only hope for a better life lay with the education of their children.

"They just didn't want the Blacks to have any kind of education," said Lanier. "I thought I would have to be a sharecropper, too, once I grew up. Just like my parents. I saw no future, I had no dreams."

Lanier's mother had other ideas, and she instilled her hopes into Lanier. A determined woman, she told Lanier that his life would be different if only he worked hard and finished his education. To make sure of this, she moved him to Chattanooga, Tennessee, to stay with his Aunt Anna, so he could attend a segregated school. There he learned to read and write and went on to high school.

As a teenager thinking about his future, Lanier looked for a way to break the cycle of poverty and do something special with his life. When he finished high school, he heard that the American Navy was calling for recruits.

Lanier was ready.

The United States was only fifty-seven years old in 1833, when a British visitor sketched a slave auction. Recalling that the United States' new national anthem praised America as the "land of the free," he scribbled a few scornful words on the back of his work: "The land of the free and the home of the brave."

During the American Civil War, citizens fought against each other, dividing the country into the North and South. The southern or "slave" states wanted to keep slavery. They fought against the northern states where African Americans were free. After 600,000 Americans died, the South lost the war, and the slaves were freed at last. But they were not freed from racism.

In the land now known as Canada, slavery became illegal in 1834, but people of African descent who tried to live there were often forced to indenture (sell) themselves as servants in order to survive.

Lanier attended only segregated schools when he was growing up, but American schools gradually became desegregated over a number of years, beginning in the 1950s.

CHAPTER TWO

Socks and Jocks

LANIER WAS EIGHTEEN YEARS old when he saw this message on a Navy recruitment poster, "I Want You."

The worst war in history, the Second World War, had already begun. Canada entered the war in 1939. When the United States entered in 1941, the American Navy and Military wanted as many new recruits as they could find. Lanier went to the Navy office and was thrilled to sign up. At last, his life could change for the better. By joining up, he hoped to escape the poverty and racial violence his family had always known.

When it was time to leave home, Lanier said goodbye to his family and friends, and travelled in the back of a truck with other African-American recruits. They drove toward the Naval Training Station to begin sixteen weeks of boot camp. Lanier looked at the passing scenery and wondered what was in store for him.

At the Naval Station, the truck drove past the gates of several barracks, and Lanier noticed that each barrack had its own name. A guard stood in front of every gate.

"You're gonna be sorry you left home," the guards called out as the truck drove by. "You had a good home, but you left," they taunted.

At Battalion Headquarters, a guard led Lanier and the other Black recruits to a room where an officer sat behind a desk. He checked their names off his list and told them about their routine for the next few weeks. Lanier learned that training would start with a few days of testing and a physical examination. Being in good health ensured that recruits did not get sent home right away. Getting fit and staying that way was first on the list for every one of them.

The barracks were segregated. Lanier and his group received their training separately from the White recruits. That first week of training was tough for everyone with swimming, marching, and drills. Lanier and the others learned about navy discipline, sometimes the hard way!

If any man hadn't shaved properly that morning or forgot to press his pants under the mattress the night before, the whole squadron had to pay for it. It was against the rules to smoke. The men must never speak to a commanding officer unless the officer spoke to them first.

If anyone forgot a rule, the squadron leader ordered the company to march around the drill hall over and over until they were ready to drop from exhaustion. Another punishment was to make the men stand on a bucket for hours outside in the cold.

It didn't take long for everyone in Lanier's group to shape up. The men were learning the importance of teamwork.

Trainers showed the men how to sleep in a hammock. It was easy to put the mattress and pillow in the hammock, but learning to lie still was tough. Lanier fell out a few times until he got it right. It took some days before he was able to get a good night's sleep.

He learned how to march in formation with the rest and managed to stay in everyone's good books. A few men did not do as well and had a hard time remembering all they were supposed to learn. These were put on the "Slagger Squad," a man's last chance before being thrown out of the Navy. The Slagger Squad worked twenty hours every day, cleaning the latrines, emptying the slops, and doing the hardest and dirtiest work in camp.

After sixteen weeks that included weaponry training, Lanier's platoon was ready to graduate. By now, the men had bonded as team members. They looked out for each other and worked as one unit. The graduation ceremony took place in the drill hall where the entire battalion paraded in front of the Admiral. As the ceremony ended, the men sang "Onward Christian Soldiers" and marched in formation around the hall.

Lanier felt overjoyed. His new life was beginning. At eighteen years old, he was now officially a sailor in the United States Navy.

●　●　●

When Lanier boarded his first ship, the USS *Truxtun*, he was dismayed to discover that he was nothing more than a sea-going bellhop whose job was to cook and clean.

Segregation was still an ugly fact of life. In the Navy, there were 170, 000 White seamen but only about 4000 African-American enlisted men. Only six of these African Americans were regular seamen. The rest were mess attendants.

"The Navy was as racist as the state of Mississippi," Lanier said about this time.

While White crew wore dress uniforms of navy jackets and pants with shiny gilt buttons, he wore a White jacket and pants with White buttons. A bow tie completed his uniform.

Apart from cooking and cleaning, every mess attendant had a battle station. Lanier's was at a large gun mounted on the ship's bow. When the gun was fired, he used special gloves to grab the hot, used shell casings and throw them overboard.

Mess attendants joking while drying their vessel's silverware. Most African-American enlisted men during the Second World War were mess attendants, also known as steward's mates.

"The mess stewards were the fightingest African-American group of any military service," said Lanier, "and any Navy Cross that was given out to Blacks was to a Navy mess attendant."

Every day Lanier shined shoes, washed the "socks and jocks" of the White officers, and cleaned their quarters. There were only a few Black sailors on board, and alongside them, Lanier ate, slept, and showered separately from the White crew.

These six steward's mates (mess attendants) were awarded the Navy Cross for standing by their gun after their ship was severely damaged in battle.

"Well they had Blacks in one place and Whites in another," said Lanier. "Blacks better not use the same shower as the White crew. You were assigned a certain amount of officers, you'd keep their shoes shined, their clothes ready, their rooms clean. You even had to wash those officers' underwear."

At meal times, he and the other Black mess attendants served at table and ate their own meals afterward, standing up in the galley. Then they washed all the dishes and cleaned up.

It was not the experience that Lanier hoped for when he enlisted.

But a change was coming. In 1942, President Roosevelt gave the order to integrate the Navy, and the first Black recruits began to take their training with Whites. It did not happen quickly but only in stages for the next ten years. By 1949, they received their training in integrated battalions, but the units were still segregated in separate living quarters.

Even though African Americans were now training along with White recruits, Lanier knew that whenever people talked about the "crew" of a ship, they did not mean the Black enlisted men. They were only talking about the White crew.

At that time, no one ever thought that African Americans were part of the ship's crew. Black sailors were placed in the lowest rank of the navy. While the White seamen worked on the upper decks, Black mess attendants had battle stations down at the bottom of the ship in the magazine—the place where explosives were kept for ammunition. They were the least likely to survive attacks during the war because they had little chance of getting out in time. They were called Negroes, and their service papers were stamped "Colored."

There was talk of integration, but Lanier and other African-American enlisted men knew they still faced an uphill climb.

Doris "Dorie" Miller showed uncommon bravery during the attack on Pearl Harbour and became the first African American to be awarded the Navy Cross.

Doris "Dorie" Miller (1919–1943), a cook and mess attendant on the battleship *West Virginia*, was the first African American to be awarded the Navy Cross. Miller was collecting laundry when nine torpedoes hit his ship during the 1941 Japanese attack on Pearl Harbour. Miller, with no previous training, fired an anti-aircraft gun to help shoot down the Japanese planes that were attacking, and he moved injured sailors out of danger.

CHAPTER THREE

Storm into Danger

LANIER SERVED THE CREW their supper in the mess hall of the USS *Truxtun*. Not many sailors had shown up. It was a rough crossing. A storm was blowing; the waves were growing higher as the ship plunged into the troughs and climbed the crests.

When he'd finished his duties, Lanier went down to his bunk to catch some sleep. His ship would arrive in port in a few hours, and then he would be on duty again.

As Lanier lay sleeping, a towering wave rocked the *Truxtun*, and the motion pitched him right out of his bunk. Some bunks nearby flew onto the floor with him, and gear and loose equipment went flying. The piercing sound of metal on rock vibrated through the ship.

He grabbed his foul-weather gear from the jumble on the floor and yelled to the other mess attendants to get topside. He felt certain the ship had taken a hit from an enemy torpedo. As soon as Lanier stepped on deck, the blast of the wind knocked him backward, and he grabbed a rail for support.

The ship was very close to land. He realized they had gone aground and that the screaming noise he heard was the sound of rocks piercing the steel hull. This must be Iceland, thought Lanier, as he stared at snow-covered cliffs that loomed above.

The *Truxtun* had sailed to Iceland a few months before. That time, he remembered the Captain's message to the crew: "Liberty for White crew, only. All other crew, stay on ship."

Lanier, three other Black crewmen, and a Filipino had gazed at the remote coastline of Iceland from the deck of the ship while the White sailors went ashore. The government there did not allow non-White or Jewish persons to step foot on their land. Lanier and the others felt the same anger they often felt when they did not get equal treatment with the White crew.

If these cliffs meant they were back in Iceland, they were in even more trouble. If they went ashore, they feared they would be lynched!

● ● ●

The ships were not heading for Iceland, as Lanier believed, but for Newfoundland. The United States had just entered the war against Germany, and the North Atlantic needed the protection of American warships. Newfoundland, with its military bases, was in a strategic location to provide that protection.

Lanier's ship, the *Truxtun*, and its sister ship, the *Wilkes*, had formed a convoy to accompany the supply ship *Pollux* to a Naval base at Argentia in Newfoundland. They sailed in a zigzag pattern, protecting the *Pollux* from German U-boats in the Atlantic. The flagship carried bombs, aircraft supplies, and radio equipment.

At the beginning of the storm that night, sleet pelted down, and howling winds rocked the ships like giant hands rocking tiny cradles. While Lanier and the others had been snatching a few hours sleep on the *Truxtun*, the men on night watch on board the *Wilkes* peered through the fog, looking out for the *Pollux* that steamed along in front. They must not get too close or the ships would collide. Somehow they had to keep a safe distance but stay close enough to be on the lookout and protect the precious cargo of the *Pollux*.

Because of poor visibility and no radio communication, it was an almost impossible task.

The ships could not communicate with each other by radio because German submarines could easily detect their signals and learn of their

The United States Navy supply ship *USS Pollux*.

presence and location in the North Atlantic. The three ships were using only light signals, instead. But the blowing snow and sleet made it hard to see the signals or to measure how close the ships were to each other.

The navigator of the *Wilkes* bent over his charts. He discovered an error in his calculations and knew the current bearings would take them too close to land. Captain John Kelsey decided to stay with the navigator's previous calculations. It was a serious mistake.

Just before dawn, the flagship's radar signalled land. The rocky coastline was closer than they had estimated. How could this be? The winds must have blown them off course and now they were in serious danger. Worse, the depth readings showed they were in shallow water, dropping from thirty-five fathoms to less than fifteen.

Captain Kelsey shouted a warning. "Stand by for collision!"

As he gave the command, a screaming sound of metal on rock vibrated and shrieked through the ship. They had run aground.

They did not yet know it, but they were in Lawn Head, a rugged area of cliffs and jagged rocks off the Burin Peninsula of Newfoundland. The *Wilkes* crew must break the radio silence between the three ships and warn the *Truxtun* and *Pollux* that they were in danger. But nature had a nasty surprise in store. The radio equipment was covered with a layer of thick ice. No signals could get through.

The men worked with frantic speed to clear away the ice so they could warn the *Truxtun* and *Pollux*, but it was too late for both ships. By the time the *Wilkes* crew was able to signal, the other two ships had already smashed into the rocks.

There was nothing Captain Kelsey could do until daylight when he could assess the situation. He did not yet know it, but his ship was not as badly damaged as the other two ships. At sunrise the crew confirmed that, even though the bow of the *Wilkes* was on the rocks, there was only minor damage to the hull. The men shifted all the cargo at the front to the back of the ship. Then they were able to reverse from the rocks and free themselves. The *Wilkes* was in good shape, but the storm was too violent for the crew to send rescue rafts to the *Pollux*. They were over a kilometer away, and in these conditions, they could only stand by and radio for rescue from the Naval base at Argentia.

At dawn the crews of the *Pollux* and *Truxtun* saw that they, too, were caught on some jagged rocks. The ships were not in view of each other and did not know the other's situation. Ice-covered cliffs towered above them. They were so close to land, they could almost touch it. But they could not get to it.

"How will this day end for us?" the crew wondered. "What kind of end will it be for everyone?"

The United States Navy destroyer *USS Truxtun*.

The *USS Truxtun* was a destroyer ship in the United States Navy during World War Two. Its duty was to protect supply and troop ships that were making their way from the Boston Naval Base to Iceland and New-foundland.

There were several American Naval Bases in Iceland. The Icelandic government requested that no Jews or people of African descent step foot on their land.

Military bases were located in Newfoundland because it was closer to Europe than anywhere else in North America. If the enemy were to invade Newfoundland, they would have

CHAPTER FOUR

Oil on Water

CAPTAIN HICKOX KNEW HIS crew and ship were in grave danger. As he stood on the bridge of the *Truxtun*, giant waves smashed down over the deck. The land looked so close, but the stormy seas and jagged rocks barred the men's escape. If the men could only use the lifeboats to plow through the angry sea to the beach, they could climb to the top of the cliff and seek help. A fence along the cliff edge meant there must be people nearby, maybe a town or village. Rescue might not be far off.

Lanier heard a member of the crew shouting for help. The man had hurried on deck without his shoes, and his bare feet had frozen to the steel plates. Some crewmen pulled the sailor from his trapped position, but this only ripped the skin from the soles of his feet. Nearby, another man lay dead. Without warm clothing,

The *Truxtun* flounders in high seas at Chamber Cove.

he had frozen to death when high waves had knocked him down.

The Commander ordered the crew to help where they could. Then all waited for dawn when they could assess the damage and get their bearings. For the rest of the night, waves pushed the ship onto the rocks, picking it up and slamming it down over and over again. The crew knew they must get off before the ship broke into pieces. The sailors were not aware that the *Pollux* was also in trouble, impaled on a rock at Lawn Head Point, in a cove not far away.

As the sky grew lighter, they saw they were in a crescent-shaped cove. The *Truxtun* had collided with a large rock on its starboard side, and black fuel oil poured into the water from the damaged hull. Slate-grey cliffs towered above. Around them the sea foamed over treacherous rock formations.

It was all hands together, and Lanier pitched in with the rest to lower the lifeboats over the side into the ocean. As soon as the first lifeboat hit the surface, a wave smashed it to pieces against the steel sides of the ship. They tried again and again with the remaining boats, but it was hopeless. The force of the waves pounded each lifeboat against the ship's side and the rocks until it broke apart.

Now only the life rafts remained. But it was the same story. The sea was just too rough. Two life rafts flipped upside down as soon as they touched the surface of the turbulent ocean, and three more broke into pieces. A sharp rock punctured the last raft.

Could they swim to shore? The fuel oil pouring from the ship had drifted onto the beach and gathered in a pool of black mire along the shoreline. Oil on water seemed to calm the raging sea. Why not try to swim toward the oil? A few men leaped over the side. Those on deck watched, terrified and helpless, as the bitterly cold sea paralyzed these men and the currents hurled them against the rocks. The impact killed them instantly, leaving their lifeless bodies to be flung about in the waves.

Lanier could see the life rafts floating upside down in the water. The men were hurling grappling hooks over the side, and after a few tries, they managed to hook a raft and flip it right side up.

Some crew jumped over the side into the sea and struggled toward the raft. They looked like little rats in the water, covered with the leaking crude oil. They climbed up onto the raft, gasping from the freezing water. The netting in the raft's centre meant they were still sitting partly submerged in the sea, but they managed to tie the ship's lifeline to the raft.

They had seen what happened to those other crewmen who had made a direct beeline to the beach. The current had swept them into the rocks. So instead of going directly toward the shore, they paddled toward the open sea. It proved to be a good strategy. The currents were gentler here, and at last, after paddling and drifting away from the strong currents, they landed safely.

The men on ship hauled back the raft, while those on shore tied the lifeline to some rocks at the water's edge. A cold wind butted them as they stumbled along the rocky beach in the early morning gloom, searching the cliff for a way upward. At the far end, they could see a rock face that was not so steep, and they made their way toward it.

Those on ship flipped over another life raft with grappling hooks. More men slid down the rope and onto the raft. It was directly beneath Lanier now as he watched from the deck. He was ready to jump overboard, but first, he knelt down with the Black and Filipino mess attendants and together they prayed for survival.

When he had finished praying, Lanier began to climb over the railing and yelled to the messmen to follow him. But the men continued kneeling and praying.

"We're going to die if we stay on ship," said Lanier.

"This is Iceland," said one. "You don't know what they're gonna to do to us! It'll be like it was in Georgia. They'll lynch us for sure."

"You want to stay here?" shouted Lanier. "We'll die if we stay here. At least we can die fighting! Let's go!"

But Lanier's shipmates preferred to face certain death on the floundering ship rather than step foot on the land they believed was Iceland. They were to perish that day.

Lanier didn't wait another moment. He swallowed his fear and jumped over the side into the ocean. He felt one quick pain over his entire body as he hit the cold water, then felt numb and sleepy from the shock. Hands grabbed him, pulling him up onto the raft where he lay for a moment in a half-stupor. Somehow the raft made it to shore as he and the men hauled it along the lifeline. Then Lanier crawled through the black sludge of spilled fuel oil at the water's edge.

Sickened by the stench of oil in his nostrils, he moved as far as he could force his body then lay still to rest. He felt his wet clothes freeze in the biting wind. Through eyes half-closed with tar, he gazed around. He was lying on a beach in a sandy cove, and cliffs towered ninety metres above him. A spasm of violent shivering shook his body.

His shipmate Harry Egner was already heading toward the cliff at the far end of the beach where other men were climbing upward. Lanier forced himself to get up and keep moving.

The two men found a small ditch at the bottom of the cliff that ran all the way to the top. It was not too steep. Lanier's hands were numb with cold but he willed himself to scramble up using his elbows and hands. Harry had trouble with the climb; his hands were so frozen he could only lean on his elbows.

"Come on," urged Lanier when he reached the top. "If I can make it, so can you."

Lanier leaned down to pull Harry up and over. They scanned the bleak landscape around them. Down a gentle slope they saw a ruined hayshed near a broken-down fence. They made for it. Inside, some crew sheltered, all of them covered with black oil.

No Black or White men here, thought Lanier. *No difference at all— just men trying to survive.*

There was not much protection here, though. They must go on; try to find a town. Harry and Lanier began walking in a direction they hoped was the right one. Lanier stepped into a deep snowdrift and fell. Feeling exhausted, he lay there thinking he would rest for a little. *All I have to do is close my eyes for a while*, thought

Lanier. He sank into sleep, hardly caring that he might never wake up.

He heard voices. "Pick him up, don't let him lay there, he'll surely die."

How long had he been laying here half-dead? Hands seized him and gently lifted him. Lanier saw a White face gazing down at him; a kind face. This person was not going to kick him aside. *He's somebody that wants to help me.*

Lanier sank back into unconsciousness.

· · ·

The one Filipino and three other African-American mess attendants preferred to stay on board the drowning ship rather than face a lynching in what they thought was Iceland. They knew that the Icelandic government did not allow Jews or persons of African descent to step foot on their shore.

The men did not realize their ship had wrecked off the coast of Newfoundland. There, the colour of a person's skin was of no importance to its seafaring people. One of these people was Gus Etchegary.

Only a year younger than Lanier Phillips, Gus was in his last year of high school, almost seventeen years old. He had lived all his young life with his family in St. Lawrence, on the southwest shore of Newfoundland.

His childhood had been so different than Lanier's.

In St. Lawrence, Gus could see pack ice right up to the shore for six weeks a year, along with icebergs, seals, and many whales. Lanier could say that, where he lived, summers were the hottest and steamiest in the United States. In turn, Gus might say that he lived on the most foggy, windy, wet, snowy, cloudy place in the whole of North America.

Gus and children like him did not have school buses. They walked to school, even though the winters were harsh and there were no snowplows to clear the roads. They did not have the iPods and smart phones that children have today. When it came to play, they just used their imaginations. There was no television, but there were snowy meadows with hills to slide down and frozen ponds for skating. In summer, children played baseball and soccer or went down to the wharf to watch the fishing boats coming and going.

Until the 1930s, the people of St. Lawrence and the near-by village of Lawn had followed traditional island ways. They fished for cod, grew crops wherever they could find fertile soil, mended their nets, went hunting for game, and helped one another whenever needed. They were a community of people born and bred to coastal life and the ways of the sea.

It was often a tough and difficult life, making a living as they did, living on a coast swept by violent seas and storms. There were as many hard times as there were good ones for the people of St. Lawrence, Lawn, and other fishing communities around Newfoundland. The people's unity and sense of togetherness carried them through the hard times and made the celebration of good times very meaningful.

Lanier was about to form a friendship with these people that was going to change his life.

The wreckage of the *Truxtun* is just visible above the water in Chamber Cove.

Lieutenant Hickox, of the *Truxtun*, remained on the bridge to oversee the rescue operations. His calmness and bravery was an inspiration to his crew. He was swept off the bridge that day, and perished in the waves.

CHAPTER FIVE

Lifeline

ON THE MORNING OF February 18, 1942, it was a "snow day" and the village school was closed. Young Gus Etchegary was enjoying the start of a free day at home, but his day was about to change.

Back at the mine just outside the town of St. Lawrence, a worker saw a strange sight. Out of the swirling snow trudged a dazed stranger, soaked in black oil, and so cold and trembling, he could scarcely speak. This was Ed Bergeron, the first survivor of the *Truxtun* to climb the cliff and make his way to the mine.

As soon as the workers heard Ed's story they closed the mine and sounded the alarm. Miners put out a call to the townspeople for help and supplies. Every able-bodied man headed to Chamber Cove. The women of St. Lawrence grabbed clothes from their husbands' closets and collected blankets and food. They hurried toward the mine to set up a first-aid station in one of the sheds and prepared to take in the survivors.

On the way to the cliffs, Lanier was one of several men that mine workers found lying barely conscious along the trail. They carried them all by sled to the mine.

Ed Bergeron, the first survivor, stumbles toward the mine, looking for help.

Gus was just finishing his breakfast when his father, Louis, told him help was needed.

"Bring the truck and get all the ropes you can find," he said. "Go on to Chamber Cove."

Gus and his brother, Theo, loaded up the truck and drove it to the Iron Springs Mine. From there they carried their ropes to the Cove where, from the cliff top, they gazed at the scene below. Sailors clung to bits of wreckage in the wild ocean waves. The *Truxtun* was tilting on her side with the port rail still above water. Men were clinging to the rail as towering waves crashed over them. Gus was horrified to see some men lose their grip. The strong current hurled them into the cliff face to die and their lifeless bodies were tossed about in the sea.

A raft floated at the edge of the oil slick. "Some

sailors got to the shore on a raft attached to a long rope," remembers Gus. "But the rope soon got all tangled up in the rocks. They just couldn't reach the shore. There was an undertow in the cove and I could see the men fighting against it, trying to get to the centre, then swim in. The other side of the cove had jagged cliffs. I saw lots of men who swam like hell and didn't make it. They smashed into the rocks and died."

Theo told Gus to help take the ropes down to the beach where his father, Louis, was directing the rescue operation. Louis gave his son the job of making a fire, and Gus found a good spot close to where the shipwrecked sailors were coming ashore. It took half an hour to light the fire because the winds were so fierce and most of the wood he found was wet and hard to burn. Once it was going strong, rescuers dragged the survivors close to its thin warmth. One of the men was without shoes or socks, and a Newfoundlander, noticing, took off his own warm socks and put them on the feet of the sailor.

Men carried over a young man without a coat, and he sat exhausted by the fire.

"Get him moving, Gus," said Gus's father.

Gus gave the sailor his sheepskin jacket. "What's your name?"

"Bill Butterworth," muttered the man.

Gus told him to hold on while he went to search for

some more wood and debris to feed the flames. When he returned, the young man had sadly died from the cold. Gus wept. He didn't know him, yet in that brief moment he and Bill had established a bond. Years later, Gus was to search for the man's family through the American Navy, and when he found them, he contacted them to talk about that terrible night.

Louis Etchegary waded into the water as far as he could and guided in the sailors. He could not shout over the roar of the wind, so he used gestures to keep them away from the dangerous currents that might carry them into the rocks. The rescuers kept a firm footing, withstanding the danger as they stood submerged in deep water. Each swimmer kept his eyes fixed on these men and obeyed their signals. Neck-deep, then shoulder-deep in the water as they moved toward shore, they knew that one wrong step could mean certain death.

In the midst of the rescue, many townsmen were thinking of their own sons and fathers, cousins and uncles in far-away places. Some had already lost many loved ones in a war thousands of miles away. Now the same war was right on their doorstep, and these brave soldiers were drowning and dying before their eyes.

It was freezing work that went on all day. The storm was pounding the *Truxtun* to pieces. The men had to work as fast as they could, no matter the waves smashing down on them, the howling wind, or the icy cold.

• • •

Of those who made it to the shore that day, eighteen-year-old Edward Bergeron was the first *Truxtun* survivor to climb the cliff. Using his knife, he cut handholds into the ice and heaved himself upwards. At the top he saw the old hayshed down a ravine. It would make a good shelter for those who followed later. He decided to go onward along the cliff and look for the town or village that must be close by. He was still feeling in good shape, and he began to jog. Every minute counted.

The workers at Iron Springs Mine brought him inside and sat him down beside the wood-burning stove. They began rescue preparations and shut down the

A St. Lawrence miner hauls an unconscious survivor toward the first aid station.

mine. They had no authority to do this, but it was the Newfoundland way to help if people were in trouble.

The people of St. Lawrence would remember that day always—the day they pulled hundreds of drowning men from the freezing water and carried them up the icy cliffs to safety. Levi Pike, then a teenager, played his part in the rescue efforts.

"Looking over the cove," he recalled, "I could see twenty men on the wreck from the *Truxtun* clinging on for dear life. It was a heart-breaking sight. Each time a large wave washed over the ship, one or two more were carried away. Some died in the oil, trying to swim to shore. It was terrible to see."

As the waves pounded the stern of the *Truxtun*, the aft part of the ship broke away, the metal torn apart by the force of all the pounding. The forward part of the vessel was on its side, its funnels and bridge under water. The waves smashed down until it too broke off, and the ship was now in three pieces and settling deeper into the water. Men still clung to the rails and gripped the line as much as their frozen hands would let them. They knew they could not hold on much longer.

Should they take a chance and leap into the sea or stay on the broken ship and wait for the Navy to rescue them? For many, the decision was made for them when a forceful wave loosened their grip on the rails and hurled them toward land. Some made it to the shore.

Others were not so lucky. The waves carried them into the rocky cliff face and they died instantly.

From the top of the cliff, the rescuers could see victims of the wreck covered in black oil and huddled on the beach. Many more struggled in the water as the current tugged them back and forth. The rescuers came up with a plan to save those who were trying to swim to shore. The wooden dory, a sturdy fishing boat built to face any kind of weather, might be the answer.

They lowered a dory with three volunteers over the cliffs and down into the water. The men rowed hard toward the desperate swimmers and pulled some of the drowning men aboard. Then a giant wave swamped the boat, tipped it end over end, and pitched a rower overboard. His friend caught him in time and pulled him back into the boat.

Some sailors had lost all their strength in the freezing water. To climb the steep cliff was impossible for them. The townspeople tied ropes under their arms and pulled them up, but the cliffs were so jagged and sharp that the first two crewmen hauled to the top were bruised and bleeding. They were just too weak to push themselves away from the rocks. There was only one solution. The rescuers must carry the survivors up the cliff face.

It was slow and backbreaking work. One by one, the men lifted half-conscious survivors over their shoulders, clung to the rope, and made their way up to the top of the cliff. There, half a dozen men held onto the rope to support the weight of those coming up. Every man they rescued was very heavy. Fuel oil doubled the weight. It was almost like carrying two men at a time up that cliff.

Levi Pike helped to hold the ropes from the top of the cliff. He could only watch with dismay as each time a large wave washed over the ship, he saw one or two more lose their grip on the rail. Some struggled in the water then became still, dying in the fuel oil and freezing water.

Newfoundlanders lowering themselves down over the cliff in search of bodies. On the night of the *Truxtun* disaster, they used the same method to pull survivors to safety.

"It was terrible to see," said Levi. "The fight to get the men to shore, the wind and the waves were the problem, blowing straight into the cove. It was very difficult to get the people up over the cliffs. So many lost their lives, so many men—two hundred and three altogether—a very sad scene. I'll never forget it as long as I live."

At the top of the cliff, the men helped survivors to the first-aid station at the mine. It was a thirty-minute walk through the snowdrifts and the weaker survivors simply could not go any farther. Like Lanier before them, they just lay down in the snow, waiting to die. The townspeople hauled these men on their horse-drawn sleds while the stronger men trudged behind.

As soon as the women at the first-aid station cleaned, dressed, and fed the rescued seamen, the people took them in their trucks or sleds into St. Lawrence. There they were in the care of families who gave them warm clothes, fed them, and tended to them. The *Truxtun* survivors did not yet know what had happened to the other ships in their convoy. The townspeople had no idea that another ship, the *Pollux*, floundered on the rocks further away.

The town of St. Lawrence lies on the coast of Newfoundland's Burin Peninsula.

Known today as the "Soccer Capitol of Canada," St. Lawrence is a community of over twelve hundred people on the Burin Peninsula. The town's soccer teams have competed provincially and nationally, playing host to amateur soccer teams from Scotland and England. Soccer is played by young and old in the town, and children play as soon as they are old enough to walk.

CHAPTER SIX

The Colour of Compassion

LANIER COULD HEAR VOICES. People around him spoke with an accent that he knew was not American. He could feel a flat surface beneath him. Someone was bathing his eyes, glued shut by black tar.

"He's all right. Let's clean him up, get the tar out of his eyes," someone was saying. Lanier felt a warm cloth gently wiping his face and head. "This is the curliest hair I've ever seen."

As soon as he could open his eyes, Lanier saw he was in a shelter, lying naked on a table, and a White woman was washing away the black oil that covered his body.

"This is the end of me," thought Lanier. "As soon as they find out I'm Colored, when they get this oil off me,

Grant Boland's painting *Incident at St. Lawrence* depicts the women of St. Lawrence tending to the survivors of the *Truxtun* disaster.

they'll kick me out of here, leave me to die, go help the Whites. They'll lynch me for certain."

"This poor fellow," the woman went on. "The tar went right into his pores." She scrubbed and scrubbed.

Lanier thought he had better tell her. She would realize it soon enough, anyway.

"You can't get it off, ma'am. It's the colour of my skin."

Not understanding, the woman went on scrubbing. "I'll get it off, don't you worry."

"I'm a Negro," said Lanier. "It won't come off."

At last, the woman understood. Her name was Violet Pike.

"Swallow," she urged as she gently lifted his head and spoon-fed him some warm broth. Lanier had never before heard kind words from a White person. She helped to cheer Lanier's spirits. "I'll take you on to my house for supper," she told him. "You stay with us for as long as you need."

Lanier could hardly believe it. These White people wanted him to live! Being "Colored" did not seem to matter to them. If this were Georgia, he knew he would likely be kicked in the head and left to die. But these people showed compassion. They cared about his well being enough to take him into their home. Was he dreaming? Had he died and gone to heaven?

When the survivors were warm again, rescuers drove them to homes in St. Lawrence to stay with families. As soon as Lanier had recovered his strength, Violet Pike welcomed him into her home. Violet prepared supper for him, and he ate at the table with the family. She used her best tablecloth and her good china, as though nothing was too much for him. When he sat down and looked at these friendly faces, all interested in him and concerned about his well being, he hardly knew what to say.

He never in his life had eaten a meal at the same table or even under the same roof as White people. But Violet and her family showed only kindly curiosity. They asked questions about him, his family, and his life in the Navy.

Lanier was too afraid to sleep that night. He was still

frightened that this was all a mistake, and he felt the familiar fears about White people. He was worried the townspeople might come for him and lynch him. But every time the door to his room opened, it was Violet or a family member making sure he was all right. Was there anything he needed? Could he use more blankets? Was he warm enough? The next morning, he put on the warm clothes they had given him, and the family welcomed him at the breakfast table.

Young Ena Farrell, who lived not far from Violet, owned a Brownie box camera her mother had given to her for Christmas. That morning, she skied to the cove where she shot three rolls of film. She was the only person to take photos of the shipwreck. She felt this tragedy was an important historic event, and she was to prove right. Later, the American forces asked Ena for her photos, but she decided to keep them for the St. Lawrence archives.

Ena came over to Violet's house, camera in hand. "Come on outside," she said to Lanier. "I want to take your picture with the other fellows."

Lanier could not believe his ears. Were they really asking him to join some of the White seamen for a group photo? The only time a White person showed any kind of interest in a "Colored" was to see how many logs he could lift for the saw mill or how many pounds of cotton he could pick in a day.

Lanier stood aside, sure that they didn't want to include him in the picture, but Ena said, "You too, Lanier. Come on along and get in the picture."

Lanier went over to stand with the others, his body tense. The other men didn't seem to mind being photographed with him. Perhaps because they had faced death, they forgot their prejudices for a moment. The kindness of the townspeople had touched them, too. They were so grateful for their lives.

The hatred that Lanier felt toward White people was beginning to crack at the edges. How could he continue to feel this way? That would mean hating the compassionate and brave people who had risked their lives to save his. Their actions washed away all his deep-seated beliefs in the cruelty of White people, just as that warm cloth had wiped away the tar from his eyes.

Why must there be so much hatred in the world? At least, he could try to make a change. He would stop hating. He would look past the colour of people's skin, see all people as equals, even if so many would not. He would begin to appreciate the dignity in every person.

Forever after, he remembered this moment as the time he became "reborn." Lanier Phillips was becoming a different person.

• • •

The people of St. Lawrence might say it was "all in a day's work," when they risked their own safety that day, but they demonstrated astonishing bravery and strength. Loss and devastation were sadly a part of their lives on this wild and rugged seacoast.

In 1929, at the time when Lanier Phillips was still a child growing up in Georgia, a tragedy had struck the people of St. Lawrence, Newfoundland. The children had just finished school for the day, when an earthquake struck. After the rumbling, shaking, and rattling of the quake, the townspeople saw the ocean drain out of the harbour. A tidal wave swept toward the Burin Peninsula on the southwest coast, causing a path of destruction in its wake. Three huge waves roared in toward land, knocking houses off their foundations, leaving behind broken boats, wharves, and debris.

All marine life in the harbour was gone, and it would be years before fishing could begin again. Twenty-seven people died. It was a time of grief and the beginning of some very lean years.

That same year brought the start of the Great Depression. The American stock market crashed in 1929, and there were no jobs to be found. Thousands of Americans, and Canadians too, had to go on welfare to survive. Jobless men drifted from the east coast to the west, riding the rails or starving on city streets.

St. Lawrence and other Newfoundland communities pulled together and took care of one another as they always had, through good times and bad.

In 1931 there came a glimmer of hope. A precious mineral, fluorspar, known as the most colourful crystal in the world, had been discovered around the town of St. Lawrence. Crystals of green, purple, amber hues—all the colours of the rainbow—were hiding deep in the ground.

An American developer was willing to mine it. Eager for work, the town's able-bodied men signed up to build a mine for extracting and shipping the mineral. The work began in 1933. The men made shallow trenches at first and worked through all seasons as they dug into the hard, unyielding ground.

Winters were the worst. At first, there were no warm shelters for the workers and no powered machines to help with the digging—just back-breaking labour. In the late 1930s, the shafts had been sunk three hundred metres down, and the work moved underground.

The St. Lawrence mine was soon to become the largest fluorspar mine in North America. Gus Etchegary was just completing his final year at high school. His father, Louis, was already superintendent of mill operations, and his brother Theo also worked at the site. Gus had a part-time job carrying telegrams from the mine to the wireless operator in town, earning around twenty dollars every month.

All the people of St. Lawrence and Lawn were earning good money now. People came from other parts of Newfoundland to work in the mines or do work that supported the industry.

St. Lawrence was booming. The miners and their families were not to know until decades later that there were health risks in working so deep underground. By the late 1940s, a growing number of miners became seriously ill from silicosis, lung cancer, and other

A building at the Iron Springs Mine in St. Lawrence was used as a temporary first-aid station for survivors of the *Truxtun* disaster.

respiratory diseases. Drilling through granite released particles of silica into the air, a dust the miners breathed in every day.

No one knew about these risks. It wasn't until years later that radon gas was discovered, but by then, the men had been working for many years in conditions very dangerous for their health. Later, mines improved their ventilation systems so that the dangers were not so great. For now, the townspeople were happy to have steady work for many years to come.

When disaster struck the *Truxtun* and *Pollux* in 1942, the townspeople were not trying to be heroes but simply following the old ways of helping one another to meet any challenges that life and the sea presented. It was a tradition passed from generation to generation for hundreds of years.

A the start of World War Two in 1939, the fluorspar mining industry grew. There was a need for fluorspar in the steel and aluminum industry to help the war effort, and the precious mineral was in great demand. The mine near St. Lawrence was the largest in North America and offered a good livelihood for the townspeople. Although closed in 1978, there are plans underway to reopen the mine.

Disaster at Lawn Head Point

IT WAS FOUR O'CLOCK in the morning, and not yet daylight. Adolph Jarvis, a fifteen-year-old from the village of Lawn, was out turr hunting in the storm. "You couldn't see your hand before your face," he remembered. Through a lull in the whirling snow, he saw yellow flares light up the sky. Had the war come to their shore? He looked over the cliff at the ocean below and glimpsed a ship listing precariously in the sea at Lawn Head Point. He hurried back to Lawn to tell whoever he could find that a ship was in trouble.

The people of Lawn had not yet heard about the shipwreck of the *Truxtun* and not many believed that young Adolph had seen what he claimed. Some decided to check out his story, however. Eight men collected ropes and axes and left at mid-day to begin the six-hour walk through thick woods from Lawn to the edge of the cliffs.

The crew of the *Pollux* did not know that rescue was on the way. Should they take their chances and make for the shore or wait for the Navy to rescue them? They could see a crack across the forward hull. The ship was about to break into pieces from the force of the storm.

The storm is too much for the *USS Pollux*.

Some of the crew fixed a hook to a line and tossed it toward the ledge of rock on shore, only one hundred yards away. After many tries, the hook caught and wedged into a crevice. They needed a volunteer to jump into the ocean and make for the ledge. Once there, he could rig up a proper line that would hold fast.

Seaman Henry Strauss decided to try his luck.

The men tied a line around him, promising to haul him back if he had trouble getting to the shore. He jumped overboard. He had never experienced such cold. His body became so numb he could not move his arms. A wave picked him up then carried him down fifteen feet underwater, but when his life jacket brought him back to the surface, it pressed over his face. Paralyzed by the cold, he could not push it back down. "I'm going to die," he thought.

He saw bodies floating in the water around him, covered in oil, and knew what had happened to them. Like him, the victims had forgotten to fasten the chinstraps that secured the life belts to their bodies. As they hit the surface, they felt numbed by the freezing water. The life jacket lifted upwards, pushing their arms up to cover their faces. Paralyzed with cold, the men were not able to move their arms back down and the pressure of the life jackets cut off their breathing.

Henry endured an agonizing struggle. "The life jacket was tied tight. That pulled me up. When I came back up I couldn't move my arms or push the life jacket away from my face. It almost smothered me. That's what happened to the others," remembered Henry.

He could only shout to the men on the ship, "Pull me up! Pull me up!" Why didn't they see he was in trouble? Then, unable to breathe, he lost consciousness. He later learned why it took so long for the crew to pull him to safety. "They couldn't pull me up. The line was so full of oil, it slipped and they lost their hold on it."

The men onboard eventually tied the rope around a winch and pulled him up to safety. Henry was hesitant to jump into that ocean again. At last, another sturdy volunteer made it to shore and secured a line. One by one, the men went hand over hand along the line until everyone remaining on board had clambered onto the ledge, about one hundred in all. About two dozen men sheltered in a cave further along the beach.

"We're out of this now," they said to each other. But the struggle was not over. All they had between themselves and death was the cave and this rocky ledge. A cliff towered above. The tide was rising. As the day went on, rogue waves began to sweep a few hapless men off the ledge to drown.

"This is the end," thought the men. Many had tucked photos of loved ones into their pockets before they left the ship. They wondered if they would ever again see their wives and children, their mothers and fathers.

The sun was setting and there was no rescue in sight. "Where is the Navy?" the men asked each other. They sang songs to keep their spirits up and prayed together that rescue might come before the tide carried them all away.

At the end of this long day, the men heard a voice calling to them from the cliffs above. "Is anybody there?"

It was the men from Lawn. They had tramped half the day, through winds and drifting snow, and arrived at last at the top of the cliff. By the light of the setting sun, they peered over the cliff and saw a heart-breaking scene. Below them, over a hundred survivors huddled on a ledge. More were stranded in a cave further along. In the cove, the *Pollux* was impaled on a rock, her bow covered by the sea and sinking deeper.

The tide was rising, and the men's perch on their icy ledge would provide protection for only another few hours. Then the high tide would drown them all.

The few villagers sent word back to the town that they needed help: food, blankets, ropes, and strong men. They began the rescue, hoping more townspeople would arrive soon. While two men at the top held the rope to support the climbers, the others climbed down to the

The wreck of the *Pollux* at Lawn Head Point.

ledge one by one, hoisted a survivor over their shoulders, held tight to the rope, and made their way back up the cliff slope. Fuel oil covered most of the survivors' bodies and added extra pounds to their weight.

It was slow and backbreaking work. As they toiled, a wild wave snatched another man from the ledge to drown. The survivors below waited, hoping their turn for rescue would come before it was too late.

Young Jimmy Drake, from Lawn, was only a teenager, but just like the others, he carried Henry Strauss and other men up the cliff face on his back. The crew of the *Pollux* was certain all the rescuers must be supermen or giants; they showed such strength on that climb.

"The whole warmth and care that they took for us was so strong that you couldn't help but feel the strength of humanity," said Henry Strauss about the villagers. "It was so dangerous for them. It was as if the whole town had no thought for themselves but only what they were doing for us. They even put clothes on us that they took off from their own clothing, because some of us had bare feet and some had no real clothes on at all."

In the inky blackness of night, the villagers told the crewmen how to reach a little wood where a weak fire was going. To their dismay, the rescued men realized their ordeal was not over. After spending all day on the ledge or in the cave, they now had to spend the night out here in the open with no shelter to protect them from the cold. They were too exhausted to walk all the way to Iron Springs Mine.

They found the place and huddled around the fire. There was not much warmth, but the light was comforting. It was so important to stay awake and move their limbs. If they sank into sleep, they would freeze. But there were to be more deaths that night as one or two exhausted men near the fire tried to fight against sleep and failed.

Some were strong enough to keep moving and decided to set out for the mine, although many had lost their shoes and their feet were swollen from frostbite.

They could take a shortcut inland, over the brush and through hip-deep snowdrifts, but they were afraid of getting lost. They took the long way instead and followed the curve of the coast.

The townspeople of St. Lawrence heard the shocking news a few hours later. Another ship was being smashed to pieces in the sea over at Lawn Head Point! The tired men had spent the whole day saving the survivors of the *Truxtun*, but there was no time for rest. They loaded ropes, blankets, and food onto horse-drawn sleds and made the journey to the cove. There they worked through the night until sunrise to bring the men of the *Pollux* out of danger. With hands bloody and blistered, the rescuers hauled the survivors up the cliff. At last, those men who had been trapped in the cave or on that ledge were safe.

It was still a long journey to shelter and warmth. The stronger men walked to the mine behind the townspeople. The weaker ones were hauled on sleds through snow-covered woods to the nearest road, where a truck transferred them to the first-aid station.

● ● ●

In total, the heroic people of St. Lawrence and Lawn rescued 186 men. The United States Navy later thanked the townspeople in a letter of appreciation. "Memories of such acts can never die," stated the letter, "and the total of almost two hundred men and officers saved on this occasion will stand as a monument to the people."

The United States government eventually built a hospital in St. Lawrence as a show of gratitude. Completed in 1954, it is known as the United States Memorial Hospital and serves the people of St. Lawrence and Lawn and other communities in the area. On its wall there is a plaque that states, "They did not die in vain."

The hospital that the U.S. Government presented to the people of Lawn and St. Lawrence in grateful recognition of their efforts to save the lives of the shipwrecked Americans.

Survivors of the *Pollux* and *Truxtun* disaster met their heroes again in 1992, on the fiftieth anniversary of the disaster at sea. They heard that some townspeople from St. Lawrence and Lawn would attend a memorial ceremony at Long Island National Cemetery in New York. They were eager to meet these extraordinary people again after so many years. In their memories, the villagers had shown superhuman strength when they carried so many men up that cliff face. They must all have been giants!

Henry Strauss from the *Pollux* was one of those who attended. At the ceremony, Henry met Jimmy Drake from Lawn. Jimmy was seventeen years old in 1942, and Henry had always imagined him to be very tall and strong to have carried him up that cliff.

"It was a kind of a shock," said Henry. "I'm only five foot six inches, and he was about two inches shorter than I was!" Young Jimmy had certainly shown the strength of the Newfoundlanders' character and determination on that terrible day.

The *Echoes of Valour* monument at St. Lawrence commemorates the bravery of the rescuers from St. Lawrence and Lawn.

Of the *Pollux* crew, 93 men died. 140 made it to safety. Of the Truxtun crew, 110 men died and 46 survived.

Lawn, at the tip of the Burin Peninsula has a population of less than one thousand people. The explorer James Cook is said to have named it Lawn because it is in a lush, green valley. The community is over two hundred years old.

CHAPTER EIGHT

The Bus to Chattanooga

IT WAS HAPPENING AGAIN! Lanier stood at the railing of the *Truxtun* looking down at the angry sea.

"This is Iceland," yelled his crewmates. "They'll lynch us for sure!"

"We'll die if we stay on this ship," he told them. "Better to die fighting!"

Lanier leapt over the side and awoke from his nightmare to find himself sprawled on the floor of his bedroom, trembling and covered in sweat. His bed covers lay in a muddled heap beside him. He remembered where he was—at his aunt's house in Chattanooga. It was the same nightmare he had every night. Only two weeks had passed since the disaster, and images of the shipwreck still tormented his dreams.

He remembered the goodness he had found in the people of St. Lawrence. His time with them had made him feel optimistic that his life would get better, that racism did not have to be a fact of life. People could change.

When Lanier had said goodbye to the people of St. Lawrence, and to the family that had taken him in, he knew he would never forget Violet Pike's

Lanier Phillips in his mess attendant's uniform.

kindness. "I will remember you for the rest of my life," he told her when they parted.

A Navy ship transported the rescued crew to the Naval Base in Argentia. There, a bus stood waiting to take the shipwrecked sailors to the reception centre. Lanier was soon facing the usual bigotry. He was the only African American survivor of the tragedy. His fellow mess attendants had stayed onboard ship to perish, terrified of a lynching on shore. Now Lanier, joyously safe, tried to board the bus with the others, but he was not allowed to join his White shipmates. There was no seat for a Black mess attendant on that bus.

He walked to the centre, where he found all the survivors were being refitted with new uniforms. All except Lanier, that is. With the other survivors, he boarded a ship, the *Virginia*, and sailed back to Boston for two weeks' leave. The crew wore their new uniforms, but Lanier was still wearing the clothes that were a gift from the people of St. Lawrence.

During his leave, Lanier travelled south to visit with his Aunt Anna in Chattanooga, where he had spent most of his childhood.

Nothing had changed in the Deep South. The schools were still segregated. The Klan was as active as ever. Whites still tried to make him feel worthless. Even so, Lanier discovered a change within himself. He now believed in his own worth as a human being. He was no longer willing to quietly accept the treatment he received from Whites. At the same time, the hatred he had always felt for Whites was beginning to fade away.

In St. Lawrence, the people had treated him with humanity. They taught him that he was a person of value, not a thing to be used and kicked aside. He tried to explain to his aunt the kind way he had been treated in Newfoundland, but she could not imagine a place where racism did not exist.

During segregation in America, Black people couldn't even drink from the same water fountains as White people.

One morning, Lanier and his aunt boarded a bus to go to downtown Chattanooga and visit some relatives there. Lanier saw the familiar line drawn across the aisle near the back of the bus—the line that divided the races. All Black passengers must sit behind that line. If the bus was full, the White passengers would sit further back, and any Black passengers must move behind or stand at the back. No "Coloreds" must sit in front of a White person.

Today the bus was full, but there was an empty seat directly in front of a White passenger. With his newfound sense of what was right instilled in him by the people of Newfoundland, Lanier sat in that seat.

"Get up, Lanier," his aunt urged. "It's just a short ride. We can stand."

But Lanier, remembering Violet's kind face, stayed where he was. The White passenger sitting behind him yanked Lanier roughly out of his seat.

"What are you doing sitting in front me?" yelled the man, his face contorted with hate as he cursed him.

Lanier felt rage welling up inside him. He wanted to hit this man. Only two weeks ago, he had been treated like a human being. Now here was the same racism he'd known all his life. He was willing to risk his life and fight this war, but he couldn't sit where he wanted in a bus. He had paid the same fare as everyone else. Why couldn't people look past the colour of his skin?

"Just be quiet, Lanier," whispered his aunt. "Come and stand at the back. We're almost there."

For her sake, Lanier stood at the back of the bus.

For the next two years, Lanier's new belief in himself as equal, simmered inside him. Whenever he encountered racist behaviour in others, the experience became more intolerable than ever. Each time he had to drink at a water fountain for "Coloreds" or ate at a canteen table for Blacks only, his sense of injustice grew stronger.

In 1943, the Navy sent Lanier to Jacksonville, Florida. When he arrived at the station in uniform, he saw some prisoners of war eating in the canteen under guard. Hungry for a meal, he looked about for the place set aside for Black customers. He knew he was not allowed to go into that canteen, but he stepped inside the doorway to ask where a "Colored gentleman" could get something to eat.

The guard on duty grabbed him by the collar and flung him to the ground. He put his foot on Lanier's neck and pulled out his gun. Lanier heard a click, the release of the safety catch.

"No Coloreds here! Get out or I'll blow your Black brains out. You know better than to come in here!"

Lanier hardly heard the racist words and curses the guard levelled at him. He only felt the barrel of the gun against his head and the seething anger so familiar whenever he encountered racism. The guard prodded him with his foot and told him again to get out. Lanier didn't waste any time.

Those prisoners of war were treated better, he thought, as he walked away. They could sit at the tables and eat their lunch while he could not. He had fought in the war against them, and yet here they were sitting comfortably in a restaurant that he was not even allowed to enter!

Hatred rose inside him, then he remembered the

people of St. Lawrence. They had no hatred. He cherished his memory of having meals with Violet's family, recovering in their home, sitting at their table. He had known people who saw no "color," only the person inside. He tried to swallow his anger. He must follow their example. He said to himself, "Lanier Phillips, that's the kind of man you must be."

Lanier served as a Navy mess attendant for the rest of the war, always wanting a better way of life. He knew there must be something more in store for him than washing dishes and polishing shoes. He determined to learn a trade and try to improve his chances. He must find a place where his worth as a human being counted. He knew he was capable of so much more.

The Navy offered several courses of training. There was a need for sonar technicians who used the science of sound waves to help detect other vessels approaching. He decided to apply for sonar technical training as soon as the war was over.

At the end of the war, in 1945, Lanier did apply. He saw a notice in the newspaper that the people had elected a Black congressman from Detroit, Charles Diggs. Congressman Diggs had overcome racial barriers and held an important government post, a big step forward for an African American. Maybe the congressman could put in a good word for him.

Lanier wrote a letter to him explaining that he was an African American who wanted to do more meaningful work. It would mean attending training classes, the course would be difficult, but he was determined to better himself.

Congressman Diggs answered his letter. He encouraged Lanier to keep trying and included a letter of recommendation addressed to the Personnel office. The letter helped, and Lanier received an order to report to the sonar technical training facility in Key West, Florida.

With hope in his heart, he stood before the Personnel officer there.

"The Captain wants to speak to you," said the officer. "Go on up to his office. He's waiting right now."

The Captain sat at his desk, papers in front of him. "I've looked at all your records. You're a fine mess attendant. I want you to be my personal steward. Come back before dinner and I'll let you know what to bring me."

"Sir, I'm going to sonar training school."

"Who told you that?"

"Sir, the Personnel office told me."

"They're wrong. Report to me before dinner."

Lanier had no choice but to salute and leave, his hopes dashed. For the next two years, he served as personal steward to the ship's Commander, but his ambition never left him. When his ship arrived back in port, new orders were waiting. He was to report to the Navy base at Key West, Florida. At the Personnel office there, he asked when he could start his classes.

"You need clearance for that," the officer told him. "The FBI has to check you and your family; see if there are any arrests in your history."

Before giving security clearance, government investigators always looked carefully at the applicant's family to see if there were any criminal records, and to make sure the person was an American citizen. For White applicants, it was a fast process. For an African American, it was a problem.

At that time, paper records were never gathered on African Americans by any government department. It was thought to be a waste of paper. Because there were no personal records for Lanier, it meant a long wait. Lanier impatiently watched the weeks go by. New students, mostly college graduates, began class, but no orders came for him.

The Personnel officer tried again to make Lanier change his mind. "You're too *old* to learn something this technical. The rest of the students are young, and their minds are sharp. You won't be able to keep up. They're all better educated than you are."

Lanier stayed firm, but the officer resorted to bribery. He would promote Lanier and give him a year's back pay.

"We've got good news. We've talked to Washington and we want to make you Chief Steward. But it's something you have to volunteer for."

"Sir, I want to be a sonar technician," insisted Lanier.

"You can't be a sonar technician. You're not a college graduate. You don't know any math. You don't have physics or chemistry in your educational background. You don't know calculus or algebra. You have to know all this to be a sonar technician."

"Then, I'll learn it, sir," replied Lanier. "I am not going to volunteer to be Chief Steward. I want to attend sonar training. Sir, if you want me out of sonar school, you're going to have to *throw* me out, because I am not leaving otherwise."

Against all odds, the FBI approved Lanier's security clearance. He entered sonar school in 1957, the first African American ever to be admitted.

The work was even harder than he had been warned, and he often worked late into the night, snatching an hour's sleep before starting the next day of training. Lanier pored over the books and charts, sometimes getting extra help from a sympathetic instructor. He knew he must work twice as hard to prove he had the same ability as any other trainee. He knew he was working not just for himself but also for those who would follow. If he failed, it would be even harder for the next African American who tried to overcome racial barriers.

Trainees were not allowed to take their books beyond the security fence, so Lanier often stayed at the school into the early hours to cram the information he needed into his head—puzzling out the problems, working through the pages of texts. While Lanier was self-taught, the other students were younger and better educated. They stuck together and had one another for support, but Lanier worked by himself, once again isolated and discriminated against because of his race. But he did not let it bother him.

"I studied harder than everyone else in that school," Lanier said. "Those other boys were there for themselves.

If one of them flunked out, it was *his* problem and *his* alone. But I had the future of Black sailors to think about. If *I* didn't make it, the next Black man would have it *ten* times as hard."

When the course ended, Lanier was eager to see his marks. He had passed! "I wasn't at the top, but I wasn't at the bottom, either," he said. He was the first African American sonar technician in the Navy and

Sonar Technician Lanier Phillips.

he hoped this would pave the way for others to follow.

Lanier boarded the ship *Bailey 713* as its new sonar technician.

When he arrived on the quarterdeck, an officer tried to send him down to the stewards' berthing with the rest of the Black seamen. "Mess attendants down that way."

Lanier shook his head, showed his written orders, and said, "Sir, I'm not a steward's mate. I'm your new sonar technician."

The ship sailed to Guantanamo in Cuba where the Navy practiced submarine warfare. Lanier was in charge of the equipment and often worked through the night to get everything running smoothly. While those around him expected him to fail, he proved himself over and over again to be a fine technician.

While sailing out of Gibraltar one year on a peace-keeping mission, his ship was rammed, and Lanier was trapped inside with other crew. He had felt for a long time that he must leave the Navy. He'd had enough of danger. However, he spent two more years teaching submarine warfare on the *Yosemite* before he could finish his career.

• • •

Lanier knew that segregation was not going away unless more people stepped up to fight against it. He vowed to step up. He applied for sonar technician training at a time when there were no African-American technicians in the Navy.

If it had not been for the people of St. Lawrence, Lanier would never have tried to challenge the system of segregation in the Navy. At that time, African-American enlisted men did not dare to question orders. It would mean trouble for them. But in St. Lawrence, Lanier had seen a different way of life where everyone was equal. He knew such a life was possible. He had to pave the way for change so other African Americans could have an easier time when they tried to better themselves.

Lanier was one of many who braved "the system" and succeeded. When at last he retired from the Navy as a successful sonar technician, he thought back on his life. He had learned so much, not the least was his experience with the people of St. Lawrence. He had not forgotten them. In his mind, he could still see Violet's kind face and feel the warmth of the Newfoundland people. They were like a bright beacon of hope to him, always offering a lesson that the world could be a different one, without bigotry and hatred.

Lanier felt African Americans had made some gains in their struggle for equality. They were gradually being integrated into the armed forces. But attitudes had not changed. He vowed to work at changing those attitudes. If he could use his sonar technical skills in a career outside the Navy, he could continue to be an example to others like him. He knew there was still far to go.

The desire for change was like a flame within the hearts of many African Americans and African Canadians. At the beginning of the Second World War, Canadian armed forces did not allow Canadians of African descent to enlist. Gradually, they accepted them as recruits but kept them separate from the White recruits. Hundreds of Black Canadians served with Whites in Europe but in segregated battalions.

In 1955, African American Rosa Parks refused to give up her seat in the "Colored" section of a bus so that a White passenger could be seated. She was arrested for civil disobedience and for defying the segregation laws in Alabama.

Many years before Rosa Parks asserted her civil rights, Viola Desmond of New Glasgow, Nova Scotia, refused to give up her seat at a movie theatre. The manager dragged her from her seat in the segregated theatre because she was sitting in the section for "Whites Only." The police sent her to jail overnight and fined her twenty dollars. She brought attention to discrimination in Canada. Her story and others became part of a sweeping movement across Canada and the United States for equal rights.

A change was coming.

The first African-American Naval officers in history were commissioned in 1944. A total of thirteen officers were known as "The Golden Thirteen."

CHAPTER NINE

A Wall Tumbles Down

THE YEAR WAS 1965. Two hundred civil-rights protestors marched six blocks through the city of Selma in Alabama and on toward the Edmund Pettus Bridge. Police on horseback, carrying clubs and canisters of tear gas, watched from the side. The people walked on, following their beloved leader, Dr. Martin Luther King.

Dr. King believed in using peaceful means. He preached that people were all brothers and sisters, no matter their colour or creed. He believed that human and civil rights must be won without the use of violence.

White citizens in the South were able to vote freely for their political leaders—a privilege that they took for granted. Half the population of Selma was African

American but only two percent of these were able to register for the vote. Racist officials prevented most African Americans from registering. The protesters wanted to be free to vote without interference.

The marchers were closing on the bridge now. Once they crossed it, they would be on their way to the State Capital in Montgomery, another fifty miles onward. They had planned rest stops along the way and knew the safe places they could sleep for the night: in farmers' fields, in barns, and churches.

The atmosphere was electric with the sense that something was about to happen.

And then something did.

The mounted police pulled out gas masks and slipped them on to cover their faces. They charged forward into the crowd of peaceful demonstrators, throwing cartridges of tear gas into the crowd. The people screamed in fear and panic, unable to breathe or see through the acrid gas. Billy clubs rained down on their fleeing bodies as police swung their weapons, aiming to hurt and disable the protesters, giving them a clear message: *You will never have the right to vote. We will stop you in any way we can.*

Police and guards on horseback whipped, spat on, and trampled young and old alike. The protestors began running back toward the shelter of a church in Selma, but many were knocked to the ground. Some lay unconscious.

A civil-rights marcher being carried away by Montgomery police.

The protestors were to know the truth of Dr. King's words: "If a man hasn't discovered something he would die for, he isn't fit to live." That night, the Ku Klux Klan murdered a White woman for helping to transport an African American back to Selma.

Marchers regrouped in a church to comfort one another, to count their numbers, and to plan their next attempt. They would try again. Television broadcasts and newspapers across the country showed the images of violence against the peaceful protestors that day. The ugly reality of racism in the South caused an outcry around the world.

This day would be known forever as Bloody Sunday.

● ● ●

When Lanier read about the violence in Selma, he knew he had to go to there.

"Those people are just like the survivors of the *Truxtun*—they need help," he told his wife. "I'm going to Selma. I've got to go to Selma."

Lanier had left the Navy in 1963 and moved north away from the Deep South with its blatant racism. He now worked for a Boston engineering company, using his skills from his Navy experience. It was here that he first met Dr. Martin Luther King, one of the leaders of the Civil Rights Movement. Lanier attended a service at Boston's Warren Street Baptist Church. Dr. King was the minister that day.

Dr. Martin Luther King, Jr. and Reverend Ralph Abernathy led the civil-rights marchers on their way to Montgomery, Alabama.

"I thought it was just fantastic; I got to shake his hand," Lanier recalled.

By now, he was further along in his dream of making something of himself. Married, with two children, he saw hope for his son and daughter. Opportunities would come more easily to them than they ever had for him, but there was much still to be done.

Black Americans now had the right to vote, but in the South, the State and local officials found ways to stop them. For those who could not read or write, officials created literacy tests that Black voters must pass to qualify for voting. Literate African-American voters might be asked to recite the entire American Constitution and were turned away when they could not. The poor were told to pay a tax before they could vote; money that some could not afford to pay.

Lanier knew these were the same kind of tactics that racist officials often used to prevent Blacks from exercising their rights and freedoms. He remembered when he had applied to enter sonar technical training school. Officials told him that he must spend two years as a personal servant to the ship's Commander. He recalled that as soon as the authorities gave him permission to begin his technical training, they told him he did not have the background skills, and offered him a bribe. He had pleaded to take the training anyway. Then the FBI delayed him because no one kept records for African Americans.

For many weeks, he had watched White students enter a classroom that he could not. Most importantly, he remembered how his persistence had paid off. He had worked and studied until he mastered the skills he needed.

Lanier believed in Doctor King's message that his brothers and sisters in the Civil Rights Movement could work together to gain their freedoms. Activists, both African American and White, were marching and demonstrating without using violence or weapons. Instead, they held sit-ins and boycotts and used only peaceful means to ask the government for change.

The song, "We Shall Overcome" became the anthem for the Civil Rights Movement. Two years earlier, a crowd of 300,000 sang this at the Lincoln Memorial after a march to Washington. Lanier had joined that march as well and listened to Dr. Martin Luther King give his famous speech, "I Have a Dream." Marches for integration swept across the United States and Canada, and the words of Dr. King's speech became known around the world.

"We must learn to live together as brothers and sisters or we will perish together as fools," said Dr. King. His inspiring words had the power to persuade African Americans that racial harmony was possible, that all the hurt and hatred among generations of people must come to an end.

It had taken Lanier years to overcome his bitterness toward racist Whites, but his experience with the people of St. Lawrence had shown him the truth of Dr. King's message that every person was his brother or sister.

When Lanier read about the protest in Selma, he took some leave from work and joined the marchers who had been attacked at the bridge.

All were determined not to fail, in spite of the danger. They must gain the right to vote freely without interference.

Two days later, Martin Luther King led them on a second march across those same six blocks toward the bridge. It was a brave show of solidarity. Their numbers had swelled to twenty-five hundred, and Lanier walked with them.

"That's the way I felt," said Lanier. "I had no fear; I had no fear at all.... I was willing, the same as those people of St. Lawrence, who came down those ropes and went out into that water and pulled bodies in, even the dead bodies they rescued and buried. It's just the humanity and the love that I got from St. Lawrence."

The bridge at Selma had been a scene of bloodshed two days before. This time, the guards turned them back, but there was no tear gas and no beatings.

On March 21, Lanier was one of 8,000 men and women who assembled in Selma for a third march that would last five days and take them to Montgomery, Alabama. By Federal court order, they had permission to march and were now under the protection of guards and police along the route.

**Civil-rights marchers crossing the bridge
from Selma to Montgomery, Alabama**

The peaceful protestors crossed the bridge and marched in triumph to the State Capital building in Montgomery. Dr. King presented to the government his petition that African Americans be able to vote without interference. As the crowd swelled to 200,000, everyone listened to his words with rapt attention. Lanier was among them.

In that same year, President Lyndon Johnson promised the people that African Americans would no longer have to pass literacy tests, pay cash to vote, or endure any other delaying tactics that White officials created.

"There is no Negro problem. There is no Southern problem. There is no Northern problem. There is only an American problem," the President said. He urged American citizens to be divided no longer, but to stand together and find solutions. He quoted the civil rights slogan, "We shall overcome."

In 1965, in the same room where President Lincoln signed the Emancipation Proclamation that freed the slaves in 1863, President Lyndon Johnson signed the Voter Registration Act. Now all American people were free to vote without interference, no matter their race.

Months later, the Voting Rights Act became law and another wall tumbled down.

Racial Discrimination in Canada

Ontario passed the Racial Discrimination Act in 1944, the first province in Canada to do so. It was now against the law to show any sign or notice that expressed ethnic, racial, or religious discrimination.

In 1954, two restaurant owners in Dresden, Ontario, refused to serve Black patrons. It showed that Canada's laws against racism were still being ignored.

In 1963, the city government of Halifax, in an act of racism, tore down the historic Black community of Africville, a pioneer settlement rich in culture and history. They separated and relocated its people against their wishes to housing in other parts of the city.

The Ku Klux Klan, in 1965, burned a cross on the lawn of the Black Baptist Church in Amherstburg, Ontario. Klan members defaced the church and spray-painted a message that read, "Amherstburg Home of the KKK."

Canada's last segregated school was closed in Nova Scotia in 1983

I'll Tell the World!

LANIER PHILLIPS AND GUS ETCHEGARY stood side-by-side, each ready to receive an honorary Doctor of Laws Degree at Memorial University in Newfoundland. It was now sixty-six years after Lanier had lain on the cliff-top path, waiting to die, and Gus had built a fire on the beach at Chamber Cove to help the drowning crew of the *Truxtun*.

The University was honouring Gus for his work with the Newfoundland fisheries and for his tireless volunteering whenever he saw the need. Lanier was being honoured for his life's work to end racial discrimination.

As Lanier waited to receive his Doctorate, his thoughts were probably full of how far he had come from that day in 1942, when he had been "reborn" on the beach at Chamber Cove. Perhaps he thought back on his life when, as a teenager, he had first walked into that Navy recruitment office. He had hoped that his life would be different, but he had never imagined how much it would change. His career had surpassed anything he ever dreamed for himself back then.

With his sonar technical training, he had worked on the ALVIN deep-water submersible team with the pioneer of undersea exploration, Jacques Cousteau. Cousteau wanted an improved underwater lamp. Engineers drew it up, and Lanier assembled the prototype. The lamps were named Calypso Lamps, after the famous voyager's ship.

Lanier had also helped to locate a 1.45 megaton nuclear atomic bomb that had sunk into the ocean off the coast of Spain in 1966.

Performer and entertainer Bill Cosby had become a friend to Lanier. Cosby was stationed on the navy base in Argentia, Newfoundland, during the 1950s. He well knew the ruggedness of that coastline and the dangers of the sea.

"There's no way when you listen to his story you hear anything but human beings helping human beings," said Cosby, who had invited Lanier onstage with him during one of his performances.

Admiral Michelle Howard, Lanier Phillips, and Bill Cosby attend the Lone Sailor Award Ceremony.

The speaker at Memorial University introduced Lanier Phillips as "one who advances the cause of humanity by displaying a quiet dignity." Lanier was a hero, and his achievements were celebrated with these words:

> *In recognition of his meritorious military service, his courageous efforts towards ending racial discrimination, and his life as an exemplar of determination, compassion and hope, I present to you, for the degree of Doctor of Laws, a hero of our times, Lanier Phillips.*

In his acceptance speech, Lanier thanked the people who meant so much to him. "To all the people of St. Lawrence," responded Lanier, "thank you for teaching me such a great lesson. You are a prototype for the rest of the world to capture and to learn love and humanity. This is a great day for me. To look around and see all these people here and see the fruits of some of my sacrifices…well, it is just great. Being rescued that day changed my life."

Right after the ceremony, Lanier left St. John's and drove with his children to St. Lawrence to attend a dinner in his honour. It was a chance to celebrate his friendship with the community. Later that day, he was there at St. Lawrence Academy Senior Prom to help graduate the young men and women of St. Lawrence as they left high school. They had grown up listening to stories about Lanier Phillips. His accomplishments were legendary among them. How lucky they felt to have this inspiring man see them off into their future lives and wish them well.

Lanier shook hands with Violet's son, Eli Pike, and other family members, and talked about Violet and that time so long ago. "I can see her right now if I just close my eyes. I can picture her, I dream of her often," he told them.

"My mother was always a person that helped people," said Eli. "Anyone who needed help, she was right there to give it to them. She would be surprised and humbled that Lanier would give her recognition like this. It just came naturally to her, wanting to help anyone in need."

Eli recalled how often during his childhood his mother told her children of that stormy day in 1942. "My mom put her best tablecloth on the table for supper. Mr. Phillips wasn't used to that. He would never talk to a White person in his life before that."

Lanier and his family drove on to Chamber Cove overlooking the sea where, so many years ago, the people of St. Lawrence had saved his life and the lives of forty-five others from the *Truxtun*. With his son and daughter beside him, he pointed out the place where the *Truxtun* had smashed against the rocks and the beach where the townspeople had dragged the survivors to safety.

Lanier visits the cliffs overlooking Chamber Cove, the site of the *Truxtun* disaster.

Lanier was never to become weary of telling the tale. "I'll tell it again and again," he said. "I'll tell it until the day I die because I think it should be told. To me, it's a lesson in humanity and love for mankind, and I hope the whole world hears about it. I just wish other people would experience the same love."

To keep on telling the story became his life's work. The people of St. Lawrence had changed his life. Lanier wanted the world to know.

• • •

Many years had gone by since Violet Pike had tended to the teenaged Lanier and wiped the tar from his eyes. Lanier's work as a Navy sonar technician had taken him to many different places around the world. He had never returned to Newfoundland, even though he had not forgotten the kind people who saved his life. He was fifty-six years old when he retired from a successful career outside the Navy. He lived in Mississippi, had children and grandchildren, and he was active in his community.

He reconnected with the people of St. Lawrence when he heard about a new book written by author Cassie Brown. Its title was *Standing Into Danger*, and he read it from cover to cover. It was all about the *Truxtun* and *Pollux* shipwrecks and the people of St. Lawrence and Lawn. He read pieces of his own story in the book, and he knew it was time to get in touch with the people who had unknowingly helped bring all this richness into his life.

Cassie Brown received a letter from Lanier that described his life-changing experience that cold day in February 1942. "When I was in the Navy," Lanier told her, "I was wounded in mind and soul, but I never forgot the people of St. Lawrence, Newfoundland. They healed that wound and I have hatred for no one. I seek no recognition—I just want the people of St. Lawrence to know what they did for me. I was healed in St. Lawrence, Newfoundland. I speak about it every chance I get. I want to reconnect with them. Can you help?" he asked her.

Cassie Brown did as Lanier requested and put him in touch with the Pike family, although he was never to meet Violet Pike again. She had passed away many years before, at the age of 63. Her husband, a miner, sadly had died at age 43 of "miner's disease."

Violet's sons, however, remembered him very well. He renewed his friendship with the people of St. Lawrence through letters and telephone calls. From then on, he kept in close touch with them.

The St. Lawrence School needed new playground

equipment, and when Lanier heard about it, he donated money so the children could enjoy new swings, slides, and climbers. He wrote many letters to the people he loved. Not a day passed when he did not think about them.

In the words of Martin Luther King, "A child exposed to racism and hatred is wounded in mind and soul for the rest of his life." Lanier told anyone who would listen that he had been wounded in mind and soul, but the people of St. Lawrence had changed that. "I just wish other people would experience the same love," he said.

Lanier had been enriched by the opportunities he was given, although nothing had come easily to him. For the rest of his life, he was to thank the people of St. Lawrence for giving him the determination to challenge himself and resist racial barriers.

"Whatever I can do for St. Lawrence is not enough. They changed my entire philosophy on life," said Lanier. "The parents there didn't teach the hatred and bigotry that the southern United States taught their kids. We're creatures of what we've been taught and the people of St. Lawrence taught me that I am a human being. It's etched into my mind like liquid steel, hot steel become cold and solid."

This was to be his message for the rest of his life.

In 1988, he read a notice about a *Truxtun* reunion in a veterans' magazine. He went to the reunion and told his story there. He told it in his Gulfport, Mississippi, retirement home. Soon, the phone began ringing off the hook; reporters, writers, teachers, and veterans all wanted him to share his story. Lanier Phillips told the story over and over again, throughout North America. Determined to let the world know, he spoke to school children, to military and community groups, and to seniors like himself.

In his efforts to end discrimination, he shared with everyone he met, and his story was soon known around the world. Story telling became his new life's work.

He moved to a retirement home in Washington, DC. On the wall of his room, he had placed the plaques and certificates of appreciation to him for telling his story. One, from the Baha'i Faith, praised his "commitment to race unity."

In his eighties, when he received his Doctor of Laws degree at Memorial University, in 2008, he was still busy travelling and speaking out against racial hatred. In 2007, he was a guest of honour at the christening of the sixth ship to bear the name *Truxtun*, named after the U.S. Navy's first Commander, Commodore Thomas

Truxtun. Lanier attended the ceremony with St. Lawrence Mayor Wayde Rowsell. There, he told his story about the good and kind people of St. Lawrence, and how they had changed his life.

The people of St. Lawrence and Lawn hold a memorial service every year for those Americans who

Lanier Phillips, Commander Timothy Weber, and Wayde Rowsell pose at the christening of the new *USS Truxtun* in 2007.

lost their lives at Lawn Point and Chamber Cove. In 2012, Dr. Phillips returned to St. Lawrence for what would be the last time. It was the 70th anniversary of the tragedy of the *Truxtun* and *Pollux* disaster.

"The last time Dr. Phillips came to visit, we met after the church service and shook hands," said Eli Pike.

"He was very feeble, he had a walker, and he walked up toward Chamber Cove."

Lanier was able to walk about halfway up the steep rise overlooking the beach. He was a frail man now at eighty-nine years old, but his spirit was as strong as ever.

Paulette Brock, Command Master Chief, the most senior enlisted sailor in the United States Navy, met Lanier that day. As an African American, the meeting had a profound effect on her.

"During the short time that we knew each other, the influence and impression he left on me will be forever with me," she said. Lanier told her of his life and experience, his obstacles and accomplishments, his joys and sorrows, "but never once did he mention the words 'give up' or 'can't.' I admire him because he stood on solid ground for what he truly believed in regardless of how much the world around and under shook."

The present day *Truxtun* is a destroyer built at a cost of $1 billion. It can simultaneously fight air, surface, and underwater battles. It is the sixth ship to be named after the first Commander of the United States Navy, Commodore Thomas Truxtun.

There is no doubt that Master Chief Brock was inspired by Lanier's story in the making of her own career. "Perhaps if it wasn't for people like Mr. Lanier Phillips, who paved the way for me, I wouldn't be at the level I am now. I am grateful for Mr. Phillips."

Not long after this final visit to St. Lawrence, Lanier received the Lone Sailor award from the U.S. Navy. It was an important honour awarded to veterans who led distinguished civilian lives after their Navy careers were over. Mayor Rowsell was there with him, and his friend, Bill Cosby stood alongside him.

Lanier Phillips accepts the Lone Sailor Award. Joining him on stage are Terry Phillips (Lanier's son), Rear Admiral Edward K. Walker, and Admiral Michelle Howard.

Epilogue

ON A SUNNY DAY in March 2012, hundreds of people, friends, family, and dignitaries, attended the funeral of Dr. Lanier Phillips at the Baptist Church in Lithonia, Georgia. He died at his retirement home in Mississippi. He was 89 years old

Vice Admiral Michelle Howard, the first African American woman to command a destroyer was there to pay tribute. She understood very well the difficulties and hard work it takes to achieve equality in the work place.

She urged women and men in the Navy and in any chosen career, who find themselves up against racial and gender barriers, to follow the example shown by Lanier Phillips. They must keep on trying, she advised. They must prove themselves and beat the competition. There can be no question of failing. Failure would just put up more barriers for others who try to better themselves.

She related how Lanier knew he must work twice as hard when he pursued sonar technical training. If he failed, it would be harder for those African Americans who followed. So many African-American women and men who are determined to cross racial barriers have been inspired by pioneers like Lanier Phillips.

Lanier's son, Terry, explained the lessons his father taught him. He talked about the situation Lanier had faced on the deck of the drowning *Truxtun*. Lanier said a prayer first, but then he acted. While the other mess attendants stayed on the ship, Lanier jumped overboard to save himself. This was typical of his father's brave spirit, said Terry.

"My father always told us to be responsible for yourself, do the work and be responsible for what happens to you. He became a sonar tech. Without his pursuit, it would never have happened. He pursued it vigorously. He prayed about it, but he did the work. That's critical for his legacy."

Terry gave another example: Lanier had not given up when the Navy tried to push him to become a chief steward. "Writing to a congressman and persisting until he was at last accepted for technical training, this was the way he approached challenges. Lanier saw the value of education and never became too old to learn or accept new challenges."

"I remember watching him and his grandson do their homework together when he was in his seventies," said Terry.

He described how Lanier took classes at MIT after he left the Navy and later studied real-estate law so he could help his family handle problems with land titles.

"My father loved education. He always worked to improve his understanding of the world," said Terry, adding that his dad worked to improve other people's understanding, too, travelling tirelessly to tell his historic story, even though his health was failing.

Mayor Wade Rowsell travelled to Lithonia to pay his last respects to Lanier.

"He was very hospitable, very kind, very articulate," said the Mayor, "noble, really, in his belief of civil rights and liberties and equality for all. I've never witnessed a person saying 'thank you' so many times as Dr. Phillips. He taught all of us a lesson in how to treat others."

Mayor Rowsell shrugged away the praise for his town's people and those of Lawn. "Lanier is the guy who endured so much and persevered, and he deserves all the credit. He certainly made a difference in this world. Do ordinary things to create extraordinary results. That is the story of Dr. Lanier Phillips."

He explained that everyone on the *Truxtun* and *Pollux* would have been lost had no one helped them, and that Newfoundlanders have always found the inner strength to help each other throughout their history, long before they became a part of Canada.

"Seafaring people respond that way. We're a people that reach out to others. We have humble beginnings but our concern for others is immeasurable," he said.

Gus Etchegary agreed that the heroism shown by the people of St. Lawrence and Lawn was just the typical response of seafaring people to the ocean's challenges. To the rest of the world, however, the skills and courage shown that day were extraordinary and attest to the strength of community among seafaring people on the Eastern shores.

The story of Lanier Phillips has become a part of Newfoundland culture, inspiring the creation of songs, documentaries, books, plays, and paintings. Visual artist Grant Boland heard the story and painted the unforgettable *Incident at St. Lawrence*, a work of art that depicts a White nurse tending an injured Black patient.

Canadian playwright Robert Chafe saw the painting and was inspired to write a play, *Oil and Water*. The production travelled throughout Canada, and the story of Lanier Phillips has become legend.

There is a saying, "It only takes a spark to get a fire going." The people of St. Lawrence and Lawn offered a spark that fuelled the fire of Lanier's quest for equality. The struggle to eliminate racial bigotry has not yet ended, but as Dr. Phillips taught, we must each be responsible for our actions; right speech and deeds are necessary to achieve dignity and equality for all.

Although we still have far to go, the life of Dr. Lanier Phillips continues to give us hope in this journey.

Glossary

BROWNIE: A simple and cheap camera in the shape of a box, invented in 1900.

CIVIL RIGHTS: A social protest movement to bring about equality and freedom from discrimination.

COLORED: A racist term used to describe African Americans.

FLUORSPAR: A colourful mineral used in steel and aluminum industries.

INTEGRATION: Racial and ethnic groups are brought into a community as equal members.

KU KLUX KLAN: A terrorist hate group that began in the 1860s. It still exists today.

LYNCH: The use of mob violence to control or punish, usually by hanging, a population of people and, in this case, African Americans.

MESS STEWARD: A member of the crew who helps with the cooking and cleaning onboard ship.

MAGAZINE: The place in the hold of a ship where ammunition is kept.

RACISM: A belief that one person is better than another because of a difference in skin colour.

RADON: A gas that occurs naturally in the environment. Dense concentrations can cause lung cancer.

SEGREGATION: The practice of separating people who have different racial backgrounds. Lanier Phillips and all children of African descent attended schools that were for African Americans only. They could not learn or play alongside White children.

SONAR: An acronym for **SO**und **N**avigation **A**nd **R**anging uses sound to navigate through water, or to detect objects such as other vessels, under the surface of the water.

TURR (common murre or common guillemot): A seabird hunted for food. It is a Newfoundland treat, often soaked in brine for three hours then roasted with vegetables.

U-BOAT: A German military submarine.

UNDERGROUND RAILROAD: An escape route for slaves from the southern United States to the north from the early to late 1800s.

Timeline . . . .

1861 American Civil War begins.

1863 With the Emancipation Proclamation, President Abraham Lincolns frees the slaves.

1923 Lanier Phillips is born in Lithonia, Georgia.

1939 World War Two begins.

1941 Lanier Phillips joins the Navy

1942 The *Truxtun* and *Pollux* disaster occurs on February 18.

1945 World War Two ends.

1946 Viola Desmond is jailed for refusing to give up her seat in the White section of a segregated theatre.

1948 President Truman signs a declaration that there will be equality for all persons serving in the armed forces regardless of race.

1954 American Schools begin desegregation.

1955 Rosa Parks refuses to give up her seat on the bus.

1957 Lanier Phillips becomes the first African American to be a sonar technician in the Navy.

1963 Two hundred thousand people join the March on Washington. Lanier leaves the Navy.

1963 The government of Halifax, Nova Scotia, tears down Africville because of racist attitudes towards the historic community.

1965 Lanier joins the civil rights march to Montgomery. The Voting Rights Act is passed by President Johnson.

1983 The last segregated school in Canada is closed in Nova Scotia.

2007 Lanier Phillips attends the christening of the sixth USS *Truxtun*.

2008 Lanier Phillips receives an Honorary Doctorate of Laws at Memorial University.

2010 The U.S. Navy awards Lanier with the Lone Sailor Award.

2011 Lanier Phillips is granted an honorary membership in the Order of Newfoundland and Labrador for his work in civil rights.

2012 In March of this year, Lanier Phillips dies at the Naval Retirement Home in Gulfport, MS. He is buried in Lithonia, GA.

Index

Image Credits

Page 13. *The Underground Railroad* (1893) by Charles T. Webber. Reproduced by permission of the Cincinnati Art Museum.

Page 14. "Children with Dr. Samuel Green, Ku Klux Klan Grand Dragon, July 24, 1948." Photographer Unknown. Image Editor. Flickr. 08KKKfamilyPortrait.

Page 15. "Chopping cotton on rented land near White Plains, Greene County, Ga." Photograph by Jack Delano. Library of Congress, Prints and Photographs Division, LC-USF35-599.

Page 18. "The Land of the Free and the Home of the Brave. (Slave Market), Charleston, South Carolina, March 4, 1833" by Henry Byam Martin. Library and Archives Canada, Acc. No. 1981-42-42.

Page 23. "Steward's mates joke as they dry silverware in the wardroom of USS *Ticonderoga* (CV-14)." United States National Archives and Records Administration, National Archives Identifier 520869.

Page 24. "A gun crew of six Negroes who were given the Navy Cross for standing by their gun when their ship was damaged by enemy attack in the Philippine area," circa 1945. United States National Archives and Records Administration, National Archives Identifier 520688.

Page 26. Image of Doris "Dorie" Miller reproduced by permission of the Naval History and Heritage Command.

Page 29. USS *Pollux* (AKS-2). Photograph from the collections of the US Navy Memorial.

Page 32. "The USS *Truxtun* (DD-229) seen during the 1930s." Photograph from the US Historical Center.

Page 34. Artist rendition of the *Truxtun* in the storm reproduced by permission of the St. Lawrence Town Council and the St. Lawrence Heritage Society.

Page 41. "USS *Truxtun*, Chamber Cove, February 19, 1942." American Legion, Fort Pepperell Post, Soiree 88 Collection. (Coll-109, 9A.01.05, Archives and Special Collections, Queen Elizabeth II Library, Memorial University.)

Page 43. Artist rendition of Ed Bergeron, the first survivor, reproduced by permission of the St. Lawrence Town Council and the St. Lawrence Heritage Society.

Page 46. Artist rendition of a St. Lawrence miner bringing an unconscious survivor to the first-aid station reproduced by permission of the St. Lawrence Town Council and the St. Lawrence Heritage Society.

Page 49. Men from St. Lawrence scaling the cliff face as part of the rescue mission. Cassie Brown Papers (Coll-115, 16.06.135, Archives and Special Collections, Queen Elizabeth II Library, Memorial University.) Photo by Ena Farrell Edwards.

Page 51. Image of St. Lawrence reproduced by permission of the St. Lawrence Town Council and the St. Lawrence Heritage Society.

Page 53. *Incident at St. Lawrence* by Grant Boland © 1996. Reproduced by permission of Grant Boland.

Page 59. Iron Springs Mine, St. Lawrence. Cassie Brown Papers (Coll-115, 16.06.048, Archives and Special Collections, Queen Elizabeth II Library, Memorial University.)

Page 62. Artist rendition of the *Pollux* listing into the sea at Lawn Head reproduced by permission of the St. Lawrence Town Council and the St. Lawrence Heritage Society.

Page 66. Wreck of the USS Pollux. Cassie Brown Papers (Coll-115, 16.06.092, Archives and Special Collections, Queen Elizabeth II Library, Memorial University.) Photo by Ena Farrell Edwards.

Page 69. "United States Memorial Hospital, St. Lawrence, Newfoundland." American Legion, Fort Pepperell Post, Soiree 88 Collection. (Coll-109, 9A.01.03, Archives and Special Collections, Queen Elizabeth II Library, Memorial University.)

Page 71. *Echoes of Valour* monument photograph reproduced by permission of the St. Lawrence Town Council and the St. Lawrence Heritage Society.

Page 73. Lanier Phillips in his mess attendant's uniform. Photograph reproduced courtesy of Wade Rowsell.

Page 75. "Negro drinking at 'Colored' water cooler in streetcar terminal, Oklahoma City, Oklahoma" Photograph by Russell Lee. Library of Congress, Prints and Photographs Division, LC-USF33-012327.

Page 82. Photograph of Lanier Phillips in uniform reproduced by permission of Vonzia Phillips.

Page 86. "The Golden Thirteen 1944," U.S. Navy file photograph. Photographer not specified. Reproduced from the Naval Historical Center Online Library.

Page 89. "Black male marcher being carried away by Montgomery police." Photograph reproduced by permission of the Alabama Government Archives.

Page 90. "Rev. Ralph Abernathy walking with Dr. Martin Luther King, Jr., as they lead civil rights marchers out of camp to resume their march to Montgomery, Alabama" (1965). Library of Congress, Prints and Photographs Division, LC-USZ62-111234.

Page 94. "Marchers on Edmund Pettus Bridge during the Selma to Montgomery March." Photograph reproduced by permission of the Alabama Government Archives.

Page 98. Photograph of Vice Admiral Michelle Howard, Lanier Phillips, and Bill Cosby taken by Wade Rowsell. Reproduced by permission of Wade Rowsell.

Page 100. "Lanier at Chamber Cove" photograph by Carmelita and Wayde Rowsell. © 2008. Reproduced by permission of Carmelita and Wayde Rowsell.

Page 105. Photograph of Lanier Phillips, Commander Timothy Weber, and Mayor Wayde Rowsell taken by Tanya Drake. Reproduced by permission of Tanya Drake.

Page 107. Lanier Phillips at the Lone Sailor Award. Photograph reproduced courtesy of the Navy Memorial, the organization which presented the Lone Sailor Award to Lanier Phillips

Bibliography

Brown, Cassie. *Standing Into Danger*. New York: Doubleday, 1979.

Farrell Edwards, Ena. *St. Lawrence and Me*. St. John's: Flanker Press, 2001.

All quotes of Lanier Phillips derived from the Maritime History Museum archives, *Dead Reckoning: The Truxtun Pollux Disaster*, Maritime History Museum 2010

Suggested Reading

Bradford, Karleen. *Dear Canada: A Desperate Road to Freedom*. Scholastic, 2012.

Brown, Cassie *Standing Into Danger*. Doubleday, 1979.

Lee, Harper. *To Kill a Mockingbird*. 1960. Harper Collins, 2002.

Ringgold, Faith. *My Dream of Martin Luther King*. Dragonfly Books, 1998.

Warner, Jody. *Viola Desmond Won't Be Budged*. Groundwood Books, 2010.

Welldon, Christine. *The Children of Africville* (revised). Nimbus, 2013.

Acknowledgements

I thank artist Grant Boland; Commander Paulette Brock; Dr. Augustus (Gus) Etchegary; Admiral Michelle Howard; Ruth Janson, Brooklyn Museum; Jane Naisbitt, Canada War Museum; Vonzia Phillips; Terry Phillips; Eli Pike; Mimi Pollow, Navy Memorial.org; Tracey Slaney, St. Lawrence Heritage Society; and a special thank you to Mayor Wayde Rowsell, Town of St. Lawrence, for his unstinting interest and assistance in this project.

• • •

Christine Welldon loves bringing little-known stories of Canadian history to life for young readers. Her books—including *The Children of Africville* (Nimbus 2009), *Children of the Titanic* (Nimbus 2010), *Listen to My Story: Pier 21*, and *Reporter in Disguise: The Intrepid Vic Steinberg* (Fitzhenry & Whiteside 2013)—have been nominated for the Hackmatack, Golden Oak, Round Table Children's Literature, and ALA Amelia Bloomer awards. Welldon makes her home in Nova Scotia.